THE YORUBA DOMINO ORACLE

THE YORUBA
DOMINO
ORACLE

Carlos G. y Poenna

SAMUEL WEISER, INC.

York Beach, Maine

First published in 2000 by
Samuel Weiser, Inc.
P.O. Box 612
York Beach, ME 03910-0612
www.weiserbooks.com

BF
1779
.D65
P64
2000

Library of Congress Cataloging-in-Publication Data
Poenna, Carlos G. y.
   The Yoruba domino oracle / Carlos G. y Poenna.
      p. cm.
   Includes index
   ISBN 1-57863-149-1 (pbk. : alk. paper)
   1. Oracles.   2. Dominoes—Miscellanea.   3. Afro-Caribbean cults—Miscellanea.   4. Yoruba (African people)—Religion—Miscellanea.   I. Title.

   BF1779.D65 P64 2000
   299'.68333—dc21

                                                                99–058153

VG
Typeset in 11/15 Minion
Cover design and photo by Phillip Augusta

Printed in the United States of America
07 06 05 04 03 02 01 00
8   7   6   5   4   3   2   1

For my friend,
Gabrielle,
And in memory of her husband Edward
and her grandmother Odessa.

Contents

Introduction

The *Domino Oracle* is an explicit divination system that has been used for many years in the Yoruba tradition. The dominos "know" their own limitations, and while they can be read on a monthly basis, they are only helpful for people who are leading stable lifestyles. In other words, they are not usually read when someone is in a huge crisis. The dominos often refer the querent to additional divinations using the coconuts, the Oracle of Ifa, or the cowrie shells, when the aid and wisdom of a priest is required. If someone using this book has no priest, or is unable to study the Yoruba tradition with a teacher, one can consult with an astrologer or a tarot reader, or one can pray to the saints. Further instruction will be given in this regard.

Domino divination has its roots in the various earth-based systems of divination that were once known as the practice of geomancy. It is possible that dominos themselves were originally created as a means of geomantic divination. Domino divination traces its origin to the Yoruba oracle of Ifa, and to the divination systems of the Yoruba and Fon peoples of Africa. While it is entirely African in its origin, in its present form it uses British and American dominos, numbered up to the Double Six. More information on the origin of these various geomantic divination systems may be obtained from *Games of the Gods* by Nigel Pennick (York Beach, ME: Samuel Weiser, 1989).

The African domino system of divination was originally brought to the Caribbean and South America by African priest practitioners of the various African animist religions. When these African tribal priests, now slaves in the new world, found the European game of dominos in use here, they transferred their native systems of divination to the playing pieces of the domino game with great sophistication. From this humble origin, and with very few changes over the last two hundred years, the domino oracle has been expanded so that it may be used as a more general system of divination suitable for use by anyone who sincerely wishes to read for others.

The domino oracle is an excellent method to teach the process of divination to a beginner. Domino divination is especially useful in all religious practices that use the deity structure of the Ibo, Fon, or Yoruba peoples of Africa. The patterns of spots on the playing pieces of the dominos resemble, at least to some extent, the marks made on the divining board by the "Father of the Oracle" as he reads the oracle revealed by the kola nuts. The oracle of the dominos ultimately originates from the same lofty place as the greater Oracle of Ifa. The dominos may be considered to be the smallest of the oracles, but like the smallest of the Orisha, Eshu, the domino oracle is not to be ignored.

The dominos have great value as a system of divination because they are very accurate in the hands of a sincere reader. It is a system of divination that may be learned by anyone from any religious tradition. Any sincere person who approaches the domino divination with the correct attitude, sincere intentions, and purity of heart, may assist another person through the use of the domino reading. Learning to work with the domino oracle is an excellent way to develop intuition.

Another reason why learning to read the domino oracle is so important is that it allows people who may otherwise not have any natural talent or opportunity to learn to read for others to enter into the art and practice of reading. It helps people learn to help others without fear that they may advise people incorrectly. This work expands the circle, so more people are able to receive the advice and guidance of the Orisha. Domino reading works to the benefit of the individual, and to the whole world.

While those of other religions may use The Domino Oracle, they may only use it in its basic form. Because this system is based on a Yoruba African tradition, more sophisticated readings will require the assistance of priests from that tradition. These priests, often known as Santeros, will usually recommend working with a guide or more senior priests known as Pardons, or Pi de Santos. These senior priests are the heads of "families" of priests in this tradition as it is practiced in the Western Hemisphere.

The priest who is consulted might also recommend other readings by a Priest of the Oracle of Ifa, known as a Babalawo. In the Yoruba religion, he is the final authority on divination.

—*Carlos G. y Poenna*

How to Read the Dominos

The procedure for reading the domino oracle is simplicity itself. There are only a few considerations that must be learned. The basic readings may be read to the querent directly from this text until you have memorized them. This is why the dominos are such a valuable system to use to teach the art of divination.

The Four Rules of Domino Reading

1. A male reader can read the dominos on any day except Mondays and Fridays. Thus, a man can read for others only on the "male" days of the week.

2. A female reader can read the dominos only on Mondays and Fridays, or on the "female" days of the week.

3. No person may read the dominos for him- or herself. A reading must always be done for another person.

4.   A querent (or client) can not approach a reader to obtain a reading of the dominos more than once in each calendar month.

The domino reading itself is accomplished in the following way:

1.   The dominos are arranged with their spots face down on a table. They are then thoroughly shuffled by the reader. The reader should then pray to God for assistance and guidance in the reading.[1] At this point the person seeking the reading, the querent, enters the reading room, if not already present. Incense should be burned, and a candle is lit to the glory of the Creator, while the reader makes a prayer to Orula, the Deity who is the Lord of Divination, that the person consulting the oracle have a good reading. A person not connected to the Yoruba pantheon might pray to his or her own divination deity, or, if Christian, could pray to St. Francis of Assisi. The prayer to Orula is in addition to the prayer asking for assistance and guidance for the reader. It is done for the querent, asking that the querent have a good reading.

---

[1] You can pray to your God for guidance before the reading, whatever your religious tradition may be. A person from a Yoruba African tradition would pray to Obatala, who, as the father of the Gods, would be called on to assist the reader in giving the reading. A Roman Catholic might pray to St. Clare, as she is known for sending clarity to those who may be in doubt. Someone working with the Norse deities would pray to Odin, and so forth.

■■■

2.   The reader now shuffles the dominos again, arranging a row of dominos (with the spots still down) immediately in front of the querent. From this row the querent selects the first domino. The reader makes note of it, and then replaces the domino with the others and shuffles them again. The querent selects the second domino, and the reader makes note of it, replaces it, and shuffles the dominos again. The querent selects the third domino, and the reader makes note of it. The reader may now either put all the other dominos back in their box, or may push them off to one side of the table on which the reading is taking place. This is done only to keep the dominos out of the way while the reading proceeds.

3.   The reader then tells, or reads, the querent the story of the first domino. The second domino is then explained to the querent. Last, the story of the third domino is revealed to the querent.

4.   Now the reader proceeds to discuss the three dominos as if they make a complete story, covering all possible details of the reading with the querent. In this last part of the reading, the remedies, including any prayers to be said, are given to the querent. Any other remedy information that may be required is also discussed with the querent at this time.

5.   If there are strong indications of one thing or another in the reading, these indications must be stressed to the querent. If there are moderators, things that weaken bad signs, or that reduce the benefit of good signs, these must also be discussed with the querent during this final part of the reading. If the

querent has chosen the same domino more than once, the importance of this particular part of the reading must be stressed to the querent. If it calls for any prayers or offerings, their importance must be stressed as well.

It is important that readers are able to give clients a remedy for any difficulty that the reading has revealed. Giving a reading that predicts difficulties for querents, when no remedy can be provided, is actually a great cruelty. In the various systems of African divination there are always remedies that may be provided for people who come asking for assistance. In the various European-based divination systems, such as astrology and the tarot, it seems that remedies are not offered to assist people who ask for readings, which is why a domino reading can be so helpful.

Making prayers, giving offerings, lighting candles, receiving spiritual cleansings, and making petitions to the deities are all remedies that must be discussed in detail with querents. It is important that the querents do what they are told to do in the reading. This must be stressed by the reader. Once a remedy is made available, querents will only harm themselves if they do not use the remedy that has been offered them. When the remedy is not used, the difficulty that the reading has proposed may be even more difficult. In other words, people should not come to the domino oracle for fun. They are talking to the gods, and talking to the gods is serious business.

Once the reading has been completed with a prayer of thanks, querents must be told that they may not have another reading for thirty days. This is always a strict rule of the oracle. In most cases, querents should be told to return after thirty days for another reading. If the reader is not working within an African tradition, and has no ability to contact a Santero or other priest for a more detailed reading, the querent may ignore the advice to do so when this is given. Alternatively, the querent may have a tarot or astrological reading, to provide more information about the situation that is presenting itself. Additionally, the querent should pay particular attention to the way in which the advice of the domino reading manifests during the coming month. The querent should also be sure to carry out any remedies that the readings may suggest as promptly as possible.

If a reading indicates that a coconut or cowry reading should be done in addition to the domino reading, then the reader does not set up an appointment for another domino reading in thirty days. The querents will be told by the priest of the tradition if another domino reading is necessary.

It is always better if the novice reader is someone who is studying with a Father of the Deity, a Pi de Santo (see glossary). A Pi de Santo is a person who has given his or her head to a deity and has become a priest of the deity. If you have no contact with a Pi de Santo, or want to study the oracle on your own, and you come from a Christian background, it is better to use the Catholic saints and religious remedies mentioned later in this book. Unless you have a Pi de Santo or Father of the Deity who is willing to work with you, the Christian saints of the Catholic religion, who are very much the same as the Yoruba deities, are the best means that you can use to assist others.

■ ■ ■

Those who come from other polytheistic religious backgrounds, such as Buddhist, Hindu, or modern pagan, may find suitable correspondences between the Yoruba deities and those of their own pantheon. Jewish people who wish to use the domino system may use cabalistic correspondences if they wish. Those who follow Islam might use the corresponding "Names of God" as remedies in this work.

If you are fortunate enough to have a Pi de Santo as a guide, you must always have your Pi de Santo ready to discuss the results of your reading with you and your querent. Once the reading has been completed with a prayer of thanks, if an overwhelming difficulty has presented itself, you should bring the querent to your Pi de Santo to review the reading and discuss any remedy that you are suggesting. The remedy given in the domino divination may be approved, or modified, by the greater wisdom and experience of the Pi de Santo. Usually this doesn't happen. I have found that students draw to them people that they can help and the gods don't send you problems that are too big to handle.

If you are working with a Santero or a Pi de Santo, you should consult them for remedies when you first begin to do readings for people. This procedure should be followed for the first ten or twenty readings you do as a novice reader. When you are ready to give the remedies on your own, your teacher or Pi de Santo will tell you. If you are studying for, or hoping to become, initiated in one of the African derived traditions, this is an important consideration.

The remedies in this book are simple enough that they may be used without any problem by people who have no contact with the African derived traditions. However, the Yoruba African derived traditions have many more remedies for different conditions than it would be possible to put into a book of this kind, so the remedies given here are only the easiest and most fundamental ones. You can safely use these remedies if you sincerely wish to remedy any potential difficulties in your life, and you can communicate this to the people that come to have a reading with you.

The most common remedies in the domino reading corpus are those that deal with Eleggua, the Mercury or Hermes of the Yoruba pantheon. He should always be thanked for a reading, and his symbols must always be a part of the household of any novice readers working in an African tradition. In almost all cases, readers who are students of a Pi de Santo should be wearing the elekes of Eleggua (see glossary) before they begin the study of domino reading. For those who are not dealing with the Yoruba pantheon, St. Michael, the Archangel, or St. Christopher may be used as the messenger deity instead of Eleggua. In many cases the querent may be given the remedy of having to light a candle to either Eleggua or to St. Michael, the Archangel, on Monday mornings. The lighting of a weekly candle on Mondays should usually be continued for at least three months. If this practice is followed, it will usually happen that Eleggua, or St. Michael, will become interested in the person in a positive way. This will always be helpful in assisting the positive progress of the querent's life.

Oshun, often referred to as the Yoruba Venus, also plays a part in many of the remedies found in the domino readings. Oshun may be propitiated with oranges, cut either in

∎∎∎

quarters or in half, and covered with honey. She may be given sweet cakes drenched in honey; she may be given yellow flowers (she especially likes yellow roses). Masculine-type women may be told that they should begin to wear skirts or to use perfume, as one example of harmonizing themselves with Oshun. In most cases, the remedy for Oshun, in addition to any others that may be mentioned in the reading, is apparent and obvious. Those who do not have familiarity with the Yoruba pantheon may use any of the milder aspects of the Virgin Mary, or the deities Venus or Aphrodite in place of Oshun.

The use of Christian prayers instead of the prayers normally used in the religious practices that follow the Yoruba or other African traditions, and the "Catholicization" of the process of domino reading will bring new people to the practice of divination. This Catholicization of the domino oracle can only ultimately benefit both the novice reader and his or her house. It should not be discouraged by those few who are so rigidly involved with the Yoruba pantheon as to see it as an impropriety.

It is always necessary to expand the circle of people who are benefiting from the guidance of the deities. One may come for an initial domino reading, and after a period of time, may decide to give his or her head to the Orisha, to perfect the guidance of his or her life, and to assist others. People who come to a reader for a reading, even for the sake of curiosity, may end up as a Yawo in the house of the reader, or of his or her Pi de Santo. We must never prejudge what the Orisha ultimately intend for anyone who asks for a reading with sincerity and a good heart.

■ ■

Reading Pairs

When there are two dominos with the same thought that come up in a reading, the importance of the subject of these dominos is greatly increased. If there are three dominos with the same thought in a single reading, they indicate the most important consideration in the life of the querent. Along with the readings of some of the single dominos, I have indicated the more common readings of the most important pairs. This will assist readers in developing their abilities as readers as well as gaining the more important information that the querent will require in the month ahead.

I have also added comments concerning the important pairs that come up with regard to the Double Blank and the Double One. These are the two strongest single readings in the domino oracle. While their modifications are legion, there are certain things that must be indicated by their connection with other dominos.

A Few Hints on Readings

The dominos you use should be wooden ones, and they should be kept in a wooden box. Dominos used for reading must be reserved for reading the oracle. If you either make, or finish, the box in which the dominos are to be kept, so much the better. In this case, you have penetrated the box with your energy, and the dominos will have better empathy for you. In no event should the dominos be ones that have been previously used in games. The dominos used for

■ ■ ■

readings should be new dominos, and they should be held apart as special for the oracle. They are to be reserved to serve only as the voice of the oracle. By treating the dominos respectfully in this way, it is believed that they will develop within themselves a sense of their own worth, and thus become a more accurate representation of the oracle that they actually are.

As with all real divination, a fee should be charged querents for the reading they are given. It is my opinion that by having querents place the fee on the altar, or on the reading table, if you have no altar, there is a more serious cast of mind given to the reading on the part of the querents. Querents may initially treat a reading as an affair of levity, or as one of simple curiosity. If querents place the fee for a reading on an altar, or even on the reading table, this light attitude toward the reading often changes. The querents then see, and believe, that this matter of reading is a serious business. They will usually take the reading more seriously. The size of the fee charged for a domino reading should always be small, say $5.00 initially, increasing after the student has mastered the art of reading through giving many readings, to $10.00, or possibly even more. The fee must be kept small, as it must allow anyone who desires guidance to come to the oracle for a reading.

Once the fee is collected, and after the querent has left the room, the fee is frequently split between you and your Pi de Santo if you have one. One-third, or $2.00 or $3.00, should be given to the Pi de Santo. This acts partly to repay the Pi de Santo for his or her effort in training you. It also reminds you that your ability to provide the remedy to the querent ultimately comes from your Pi de Santo.

It is hoped that this brief discussion of reading the domino oracle will interest you in developing your ability to read for others, and to perfect yourself by learning this very worthwhile art.

CHAPTER 2

■ ■ ■

What Each
Domino Means

Double Blank

This is one of the worst of the domino readings. It announces the presence of deceit and treachery in the querent's life. If he or she has gained, received, or acquired anything through the use of fraud, deceit, or treachery, he or she will keep it. However he or she will pay for these acts of fraud, deceit, and treachery with tears and suffering. This reading announces to the querent that there will be losses in business, upsets in the love life, and the possible loss of a job, or a position in life. These upsetting experiences are the ultimate result for the person who receives this domino in a reading. This is a strong admonition that the querent must heed this warning or suffer the consequences.

If this reading does not seem to apply to the querent, the reading becomes a warning of the possibility of an impending accident. The querent should pray to the deities Oya and Chango

(St. Barbara) immediately, asking them in prayer to moderate, or divert, the impending accident. See glossary for details.

Double Blank is always a very negative reading, announcing that the person who is consulting the oracle must turn away from deceit and treachery immediately. The person is being warned to change his or her ways. The person is in danger of divine justice and retribution falling on him or her unless a change in lifestyle takes place immediately. Whatever the deed—the time has come to make amends for these actions. This especially applies to anything gained through fraud, deceit, or treachery. Unless the person is willing to make amends, and has a sincere desire for repentance and forgiveness, there are grave difficulties ahead.

Double Blank with Double One

Double Blank is moderated favorably only by the **Double One.** If these two come up in a reading, it is a sign that the querent must make a choice in the coming month as to which path in life to follow. The querent will be given a choice during the month to come between the path of good and that of evil. The querent must ask the reader or the reader's Pi de Santo for guidance when this choice presents itself. Such choices are not always as obvious as we might like them to be.

There is a very strong contrast here between the good of the **Double One** and the bad of the **Double Blank.** The querent should be questioned as to how he or she views the progress of life to this point in time. If the querent has a positive attitude, and if life has been going well, there is only the matter of paying back (or restoring) others for any harm done by any previous treachery that may have been committed, or for anything that may have been received through fraud and deceit.

This reading is an indication that the person is about to be faced with the judgment of Chango. The querent must search his or her heart to find out just what must be done to restore to others what has been taken from them. At the very least, the querent should place a substantial sum, equal to about a week's income, in the poor box of his or her church or temple. Prayers to Chango and the feeding of the head should be done after this restitution has been made (see glossary).

The person who has been rewarded by life, but who still maintains a negative attitude is not in so fortunate a position. This person must repay the various Orisha (deities or saints) for the gifts given in life, and must seek to repay all of those who have been harmed. The querent who is negative-minded is not likely to want to do this. If the querent does not at least begin to make restitution this month, disaster may befall this person as he or she has been warned by the Orisha in this reading.

It is the difficult task of the reader to inform the querent that he or she owes this repayment to others. The querent must be informed restitution is necessary or the coming time of judgment will leave the querent in very poor straits indeed. The querent is being given a warning with this reading, but while it is not as strong a warning as the **Double Blank** alone, it is a definite warning that the wise person will heed. This reading shows the two sides of the coin of life—the good and the bad. The person consulting the oracle must choose which he or she will follow.

■ ■ ■

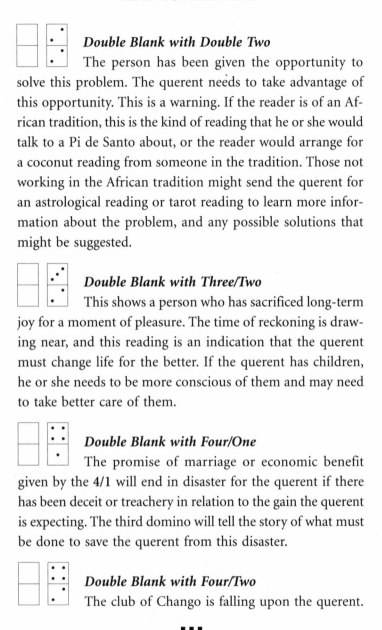

Double Blank with Double Two

The person has been given the opportunity to solve this problem. The querent needs to take advantage of this opportunity. This is a warning. If the reader is of an African tradition, this is the kind of reading that he or she would talk to a Pi de Santo about, or the reader would arrange for a coconut reading from someone in the tradition. Those not working in the African tradition might send the querent for an astrological reading or tarot reading to learn more information about the problem, and any possible solutions that might be suggested.

Double Blank with Three/Two

This shows a person who has sacrificed long-term joy for a moment of pleasure. The time of reckoning is drawing near, and this reading is an indication that the querent must change life for the better. If the querent has children, he or she needs to be more conscious of them and may need to take better care of them.

Double Blank with Four/One

The promise of marriage or economic benefit given by the 4/1 will end in disaster for the querent if there has been deceit or treachery in relation to the gain the querent is expecting. The third domino will tell the story of what must be done to save the querent from this disaster.

Double Blank with Four/Two

The club of Chango is falling upon the querent.

■ ■

The changes promised by the 4/2 will be negative unless something is done immediately. If the reader is working in the African tradition, their Pi de Santo or Padrino should be consulted about this reading. In some cases nothing can be done to avert the coming blows.

Double Blank with Five/Blank

The querent must be careful about a member of the opposite sex who is coming into his or her life. This person may well ruin the querent's life. This combination always indicates the possibility of venereal infection from the sexual partner during the coming month.

Double Blank with Five/One

This combination indicates that there is a potential to lose everything through a member of the opposite sex. Both men and women who receive this reading must observe the Oshun taboos for at least the next three months. If the reader is working within the African tradition, a coconut reading is indicated. If the reader comes from another tradition, the reader should advise the querent to obtain a tarot reading, or an astrological reading, concerning his or her relationships with the opposite sex.

Double Blank with Five/Three

This reading moderates the difficulty of the **Double Blank** once reparations are made by the querent. Chango is watching, but his club is at his side, not raised to strike as yet.

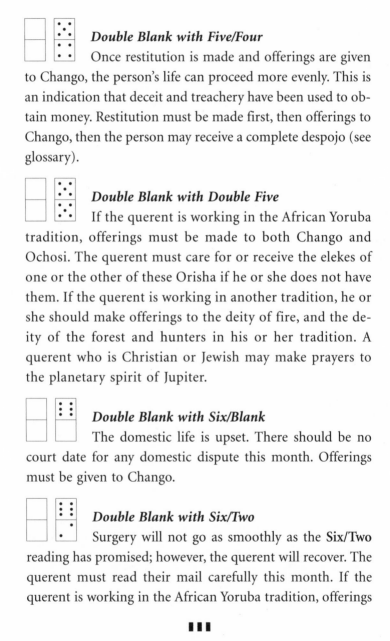

Double Blank with Five/Four

Once restitution is made and offerings are given to Chango, the person's life can proceed more evenly. This is an indication that deceit and treachery have been used to obtain money. Restitution must be made first, then offerings to Chango, then the person may receive a complete despojo (see glossary).

Double Blank with Double Five

If the querent is working in the African Yoruba tradition, offerings must be made to both Chango and Ochosi. The querent must care for or receive the elekes of one or the other of these Orisha if he or she does not have them. If the querent is working in another tradition, he or she should make offerings to the deity of fire, and the deity of the forest and hunters in his or her tradition. A querent who is Christian or Jewish may make prayers to the planetary spirit of Jupiter.

Double Blank with Six/Blank

The domestic life is upset. There should be no court date for any domestic dispute this month. Offerings must be given to Chango.

Double Blank with Six/Two

Surgery will not go as smoothly as the **Six/Two** reading has promised; however, the querent will recover. The querent must read their mail carefully this month. If the querent is working in the African Yoruba tradition, offerings

■ ■ ■

must be made to both Chango and Obatala. If the querent is working in another tradition, he or she should make offerings to both the deity of fire, and the highest deity, or father deity, in his or her tradition. Those who are either Christian or Jewish may make prayers to the planetary spirit of Jupiter and the planetary spirit of the Sun.

Double Blank with Six/Three
The person who is separated from his or her beloved will not find that any reconciliation is possible this month. Should it appear to be taking place, the reconciliation will be one that does not last.

Double Blank with Six/Four
This reading is often a sign that negative work has been done on the querent. The reader who is working in the African Yoruba tradition should take the querent to a Pi de Santo immediately. The reader who is working in other traditions should seek the advice of a priest or priestess in that tradition so that a spiritual cleansing from that tradition can be performed upon the querent. This negative work can be removed.

One/Blank

The **1/Blank** domino is always set aside and not read. It may be removed from the set if desired. It seems that Olofi would be speaking through the 1/Blank. It may also be that it is not read because it is taken for his symbol, the symbol of One God, the Creator, who is always viewed as being above all of the flux of human changes on the earth.

Double One

This is one of the best of the domino readings. The 1/1 indicates happiness, both in the querent's love life and in business affairs. There is a promise of harmony in the home, as well as harmony in the business, or a job. The querent who is single may even have the promise of a lover and possibly eventual matrimony this month. In the realm of business affairs, this reading indicates triumph in the person's affairs, as well as economic security for the coming month.

The 1/1 is a very positive reading, indicating that the affairs of the querent are in good order and are progressing well. The querent should give a thanks offering to the deity of his or her head, if the querent knows who it is. Prayers of thanks to God or Olofi should also be offered. If the querent does not know the deity of his or her head, prayers of thanksgiving to God should be made on a regular daily basis in the coming month. The querent should also maintain the positive mental attitude gained this month throughout the life. The querent is presently listening to good intuition, and must continue to do so. Notice that this reading says nothing about health. However, receiving this domino in a reading adds to the benefits promised in any reading calling for better health, and it moderates any evil prediction that may be indicated

■ ■

in another part of the reading. This reading is especially positive for love and money, but it is also generally positive for everything else in the person's life.

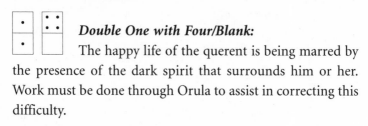

Double One with Double Blank
See **Double Blank**, page 13.

Double One with Double Two
This is an indication that the affairs of the querent are going very well indeed. There is a caution in the **2/2** that an older man may become an obstacle to the querent's progress this month. There are Orisha (saints or deities) who are standing by to assist the querent. The querent must be prepared to recognize these forces, and ask for their help.

Double One with Three/Two
This pair is always an indication that the person should play the lottery in the coming month. The querent is living in a streak of luck and should take advantage of it, being grateful and generous in return to those around.

Double One with Four/Blank:
The happy life of the querent is being marred by the presence of the dark spirit that surrounds him or her. Work must be done through Orula to assist in correcting this difficulty.

Double One with Four/One
Another indication of a favorable opportunity in the month to come. The querent should play the lottery this month.

■■■

Double One with Four/Two
The coming changes will be quite favorable for the querent. The offerings of food and music must be made, and sincere gratitude should be expressed, once the favorable changes have manifested.

Double One with Five/Blank
An indication of an adulterous union that will not be discovered this month. The affair is safe for the month following the reading in any event. The possibility of a serious accident to the querent is also reduced.

Double One with Five/One
This is a gentle reminder from Oshun that she has given favors to the querent, and that she would like offerings and recognition in return.

Double One with Five/Three
This combination deals with the querent's economic evolution. Nothing is required at this time, but prayers of thanksgiving should be made, to continue the upward progress of the querent's economic life.

Double One with Five/Four
The affectionate life will improve greatly this month. However, caution in investing money is advised.

Double One with Double Five
The affectionate life is stressed, and the querent

should make an Ebo for Ochosi, or place his symbol in the home to be certain that the promised benefits arrive.

Double One with Six/Blank

The querent will hear of a happy marriage this month. There will be a beneficial impact on the querent from the event. Good is in prospect this month.

Double One with Six/Two

The querent will have a very good month, and should take advantage of it.

Double One with Six/Three

Love and romance are accented this month. The querent will have a very good month, and should take advantage of it.

Double One with Six/Four

The individual's time of troubles is over. The way is opened to them this month for ultimate happiness and joy. Whatever was blocking the querent has been removed, and life will now move forward. This pair is an assurance of victory ahead.

Two/Blank

This domino is an indication of treachery and bad luck in the life of the querent. If a woman is questioning the oracle, she must be careful when dealing with her husband or her boyfriend. If the querent is considering traveling, or changing environment, he or she should plan to actually make the change, as it will be a favorable. Oshun is asking for a substantial offering. A piece of plain cake drenched in honey, along with five pennies, should be given to her, preferably by placing the offering in the flowing waters of a river.

Two/Blank is an indication that the person's life is turning this month. However, the manner in which the life will turn is not yet to be revealed. If the querent is a woman, the lovers and the friends of this woman must be examined now. Ask her about these lovers and friends, make a list of their names. If one of them is the person who will betray or harm her, the name of the person will stand out on the list. Ask the woman if she has ever had any lovers beside her husband or her boyfriend. This information from the woman's past will be of importance.

If the domino falls with the 2 facing the reader, and the querent is a man, there is not as much difficulty forecast in the life, but the life is still in the process of changing. In this case, a move, or even a change of the querent's environment is indicated to be more desirable. If moving, changing positions, or occupations, is a question in the mind of a male querent, it is a confirmation that it will be advisable for him to make these changes.

Whatever the other considerations, the offering that has been asked for by Oshun should be given to her at a river whenever possible. The offering must be made within five days after the reading. In addition, prayers of thanks should be said to Oshun. These prayers should be made after lighting a yellow candle to her every day for five days.

■ ■ ■

A female querent who has had sex with more men than she is years old must make prayers to Oshun after lighting yellow candles to her for five consecutive days. This is in addition to making the offering Oshun has requested at a river. This work is required to turn aside the potential betrayal that was forecast for the querent in the reading.

The prayers to Oshun are particularly necessary in the case of a married woman who either has cheated on her husband, or who was sexually promiscuous before she married him. This reading always indicates a woman who does not treat her husband or her boyfriend well. She must change her attitude about the man in her life during the coming month. She must treat the man she is with better than she has treated other men she has been intimate with in the past. The reader should advise the woman as to what to do about this, depending upon the circumstances of her particular case.

Two/Blank with Two/One
This is a very direct threat to the health of the man in the life of a woman querent. If the reader is working within the African tradition, a coconut reading is indicated. If the reader comes from another tradition, the reader should advise them to obtain a tarot reading, or an astrological reading, concerning their relationship.

Two/Blank with Four/Blank
Men whom the woman may meet in the next six weeks are probably not well disposed toward her. She should be cautious about any new man in her life.

Two/Blank with Five/Blank

The querent may believe that he or she is free to do as he or she pleases, but this is not true. A despojo (spiritual cleansing) is indicated.

Two/One

For the single woman querent, this reading is an indication of an upcoming marriage. This domino always shows a marriage that brings economic stability into her life. However, this domino also shows that the first marriage may also bring widowhood, separation, or divorce from her husband at an early age. The woman's first marriage will then be followed by a second marriage that will last for many years.

The married woman who consults this oracle should be careful concerning her husband's health. Her husband is in danger of a sickness, which may be followed by sudden death. If the querent is a married woman, she must do all that she can to take care of her husband's health, and preserve his welfare.

The same readings concerning economic stability in the marriage also apply to the man who consults the oracle. However, the man who consults the oracle must also be made aware that there is someone around him who envies him. He must be aware of those who are jealous of his position in life. The man who selects this domino should also be careful with money, as he may lose some money or even be robbed

■ ■ ■

in the coming month. It is recommended that a charm or talisman be prepared, to protect the querent against harmful effects of these negative influences.

The single woman querent must be careful of the man she marries. It is much better if the man she marries is older than she is, as a marriage to a younger man will not be as happy for her. If the 2 falls toward the querent, male or female, it shows more chance of a happier union than if it is the 1 that falls closer to the querent. The 1 toward a single female querent shows an earlier widowhood, or an early separation from the man she marries. The married woman querent is being warned in this reading to go out of her way to be particularly good to her husband. She must make great efforts to extend herself for him, and to be very caring of him.

If the woman querent has "Made the Saint," an initiation into the African tradition, she may obtain a "Cup of Osainyin" (a charm) from her Pi de Santo if his reading indicates that it is needed. If she wishes to avert her husband's illness, she must consult her Pi de Santo for his counsel. If she has not "Made the Saint," she should pray to Osainyin, or St. Francis of Assisi, for aid. Once her husband falls sick, and all during his illness, she must be certain that he receives the best possible care from her hands.

The male querent who receives this reading will usually require a despojo, a full spiritual cleansing. If this is the case, he should receive it at once. He should also receive an asavache, or a charm, to protect him against malochia induced by the jealousy or envy of others. If the man has made investments, there is a good chance that they are not stable, or that they are not being managed properly. This is always a

■ ■ ■

warning for the male querent to check on the state of his investments. The querent should also protect the home against robbery. If it is desired, a charm may be prepared for this protection.

Two/One with Four/Blank
This indicates a potentially serious difficulty, which may be identified and possibly remedied through a more detailed reading.

Two/One with Four/Three
This is a very encouraging reading. The information given under 2/1 must be followed to have the best outcome.

Two/One with Five/Blank
There is a serious threat of slander and disgrace present concerning the woman's relationships with men. She should avoid consorting with a married man, as such an opportunity may present itself to her this month. This relationship would end in great difficulty and slander directed against her.

Double Two

Triumph in business, and great happiness, will be available in all that the querent undertakes this month. The twin deities (Ibeji) speak of a business trip to another town. But there is an older man there who may be-

come an obstacle to the querent. If the querent has not received elekes, he or she should receive a reading from a Pi de
Santo. If no Pi de Santo is available, he or she should work
with the Prayer to the Divine Warriors (p. 54) or the Prayer
to the Seven African Powers (p. 75). And if no Pi de Santo is
available, the querent may want to pursue an astrological or
tarot reading for further direction. The spiritual path has
opened to this person.

If the querent comes from the Yoruba tradition, he or
she needs to obtain a cowrie reading from a Pi de Santo. If
the querent has received elekes (necklaces of the deity), the
querent must "feed" them. If the querent has elekes, he or
she should be wearing them when the cowrie reading is done
by the Pi de Santo. The querent should also say prayers to
the Warriors (p. 54) or to the Seven African Powers (p. 75)
according to the way that the querent will be instructed by
the Pi de Santo. All of the querent's future development will
depend upon successfully accomplishing these prayers.

This reading promises success to the person who is following a spiritual path, and who is attentive to it. It is also
a reminder that every person should follow a spiritual path
of some kind. If the querent has begun to follow a spiritual path, whether it is in the African tradition or not, he
or she is being gently reminded that if he or she has strayed
from the path, it is time to return to it. While the querent
is not in any difficulty with the deities of that path, it is a
warning that the querent is off the path. The querent is
being reminded that we each must develop ourselves to
the best of our abilities. As this system of divination is
based on the African tradition, the information in this

section applies to that tradition. The caution about going on a spiritual path, and staying on it, however, applies to everyone.

In many cases the Orisha who rules the querent's head and the Orisha of the occupation, or of the goal in life, should own the elekes given to the querent. A prayer for daily use may be given the querent, if the reader desires to do so. In this case it will usually be a prayer to God, Obatala, or to Olofi. The Lord's Prayer, or the 23d Psalm, may also be used as a daily prayer for this purpose. This is to be done in addition to the prayer to the Warriors, which is required in the reading. In some cases this reading indicates that a person has entered on a spiritual or devotional path. It indicates that the querent has been off this path for a time. This reading is telling the querent to get back to work on the spiritual or devotional path, but it is telling the querent in a gentle way. It is often appropriate to ask the querent how long it has been since he or she has been to church.

Double Two with Double One
See under 1/1.

Three/Blank

This domino is an indicator of quarrels, arguments, and fights. For a man, this reading often indicates that he has a wife with a bad temper. This is an indication that the man is married to a woman who argues with him continually. She would really like to ask him for a divorce. He should give her a divorce, as she is not either an honest or a sincere woman. The querent must avoid going to bars, and listening to, or participating in, gossip of any kind. He should avoid spending time in any places that are cloaked in darkness. On the Monday following the reading, the querent must give a substantial offering to Eleggua, and he should light a candle to Eleggua as well. If the reader is working within the African tradition, a coconut reading is indicated so that Eleggua can tell him what is to be done to overcome all of his problems. If the reader comes from another tradition, the reader should advise the querent to obtain a tarot reading, or an astrological reading, concerning relationships with the opposite sex. In any event, counseling the querent concerning relationships is strongly recommended.

The male querent in the African tradition who receives this reading may legitimately ask to have his wife placed under his control. A Pi de Santo can do this if his coconut or cowry reading indicates that it is either advisable or necessary. The querent may also legitimately ask the Pi de Santo that something be done to rid himself of his wife, by making her decide to leave him.

If the male querent is not married, this reading is a strong warning to him that he must be very careful in entering into marriage. He must also be advised to be very careful in all his other relationships with women, as well. The single male querent must avoid involvement with any women he meets, or has met, in a bar, club, or in any of the "places cloaked in darkness" mentioned in the read-

■■■

ing. He should also be cautious of all women who come into his life in any other way during this month.

The nature of the female querent is frequently described by the reading of the wife as it is given above. In this case, the reader should be aware that the woman who is consulting him is not really sincere. In all cases the querent should be taught how to make weekly offerings to Eleggua, St. Michael, or St. Christopher. She should make these offerings for at least the next three months. Ideally the offerings should be made more regularly, for an even longer period of time, say for a year or so. This particular reading is almost a command from Eleggua to make the offerings. The offerings should be made beginning the Monday following the reading.

Three/Blank with Six/Six

This person is being told to practice both regular prayers and frequent church attendance. The querent must become more sincere in life.

Three/One

This domino is a warning of both danger to the querent, and of a potential problem with the law. Someone is coming to the querent bearing bad news, but the querent will be able to resolve the problem that is approaching. However, the querent must be more careful with a matrimonial problem than a business difficulty. Eleggua is causing problems in the house. He feels that he has been abandoned. If the querent does not have Eleggua in the home, he should be brought there as soon as possible. The querent should light a candle to Eleggua on Mondays, and give him an offering each week. The reader will instruct the querent about the details of the offering.

This is another request from Eleggua for weekly offerings. The querent should also have his or her head fed and blessed if it has not been done, or if it has not been done within the past year. It is necessary that the querent be able to think his or her way through any coming problem, and not respond to the problems that are presented with emotion and rage. Inquiry into the kind of matrimonial problem that is indicated may be done with the coconut reading if you can arrange one (or an astrological or a tarot reading), but if not, the querent will usually already have some idea of what the matrimonial or relationship problem is about.

If any other domino is picked in the reading that indicates a matrimonial or relationship problem, the seriousness of this problem is magnified greatly. This makes any indications of a coming divorce or separation more likely.

There seems to be something that has been left undone when this domino is selected. Ask the querent if something was started and abandoned before completion. It may be an uncompleted project, or an unfulfilled promise to someone. If this is revealed by the querent, whatever it may be, that which is undone must be completed as soon as possible.

This is often a sign that the querent is not doing all that can be done in some area of life. It may be that the querent is holding back on the job, or is unwilling to be of assistance to others.

■ ■ ■

Three/Two

This domino indicates a fortunate combination in love, as well as success in business. The deities accompany the querent, but he or she must remember to thank them more often. The querent must also feed the deities more regularly. It is a good time for business, romance, and even matrimony. The querent will be fortunate in games, and in gambling, this month. Children must be given more attention. The querent's children are not well disposed to the querent, because he or she does not spend enough time with them.

If the querent is a man with sons, he must talk to his children more often, and play with them, as well. He has not taught them about the world, and this will cause them to suffer in the future. A woman who has daughters must do the same, as the problem is exactly the same. This reading shows that there is an order or system in the querent's life that is working out to his or her advantage. The querent should make prayers of thanksgiving to God or Olofi. If the querent has elekes, he or she must be particularly careful to feed the deities and to care for the elekes.

This domino is always an indication that the querent should play the lottery during the coming month. The indication that this month will be favorable to the querent's business or matrimony is an indication that it is a good time to begin either. It is also a time to look for advancement or improvement in either the business or matrimonial situation.

Double Three

This is one of the best domino readings. It always indicates that a large amount of money will unexpectedly come into the querent's life. A visit will take place from a good friend who brings gifts to the querent. The querent will recover from an illness that he or she may have had for some time. There may also be a reunion with a friend, or a family member, who comes from a long distance. Things are going very well, and all of the querent's affairs are prospering. Eleggua is standing strong at the querent's doorway.

This reading shows that there is a blessing of money coming—not just a small gift, or a casual action that brings in a little money. If there are no other resources in sight, the querent should play the lottery, as well as wait in thanksgiving for the promised money to arrive. This reading always indicates a positive change in the conditions surrounding the querent. The nature of these changes is only outlined above; the changes may include other areas of the person's life, as well.

Four/Blank

This domino indicates that there is unhappiness in the querent's love life. If the querent is engaged to be married, it reveals that the marriage will not come to pass. The querent will be involved in gossip, as well as with emotional problems with other people. For the pregnant woman, this domino reading signifies the chance of twins or triplets, but often a difficult birth may also be in store. In some cases, it may be an indication of a premature baby. The querent should go to Orula for help with problems, as there is a very dark spirit following him or her.

This reading always indicates that there is a stagnant condition around the person that must be broken up to allow the life to move forward. The symbol is that of stagnant water around a log jam. The person requires a major despojo and a feeding of the head as well as a blessing. Usually this work should be done by a Pi de Santo, or a priest or priestess of the reader's tradition.

If this domino should come up with a reading indicating elekes, it becomes almost a threat that something must be done to help the querent immediately. The removal of the dark spirit from the person should follow as soon as possible. This dark spirit is the major source of the querent's problems at the present time.

For the married querent, this domino often indicates a coming divorce or separation. If this reading occurs with another domino promising divorce or separation, it is a guarantee that the time of the querent's marriage is over.

Ask the querent if he or she feels the presence of darkness around. If this is true, inquire into it and let the querent speak about it to you. The querent will tell the reader the story of the true difficulty.

Pregnant women who choose this domino in a reading must be placed under the protection of one of the deities, either Yemenja or Oshun in most cases. A bath for either of them

I I I

may be of assistance. Osainyin must be consulted to find out if the child or children can be born safely. Those not working in an African tradition may use the maternal deity in their tradition and the deity of medicine or healing to pray for the protection of the mother and the child. Christians should pray to the Virgin Mary and St. Rafael, the Archangel, for this work.

If there has been a recent death in the querent's family, and if you are working in the African tradition, the wristlet of Orula should be given the querent by a Pi de Santo. The need for it may be confirmed by the coconuts, or by the Pi de Santo. If the difficulty is severe, as shown by the coconut reading, it may be necessary to get a reading from a Diviner of the Oracle of Ifa. Work through Orula to remove the dark spirit surrounding the querent. This must be done before consulting a Diviner. If you come from another tradition, you should make prayers to the deity of death, or to the principle deity of the tradition, for it is necessary that the querent remove the dark influence from his or her life, in order to continue to live a successful life on Earth.

Four/Blank with Four/Three

This is a testimonial of the obstacles that lie in the path of a woman querent's life. However, this is also a testimonial that these obstacles may be removed. The woman querent should receive a despojo and a feeding of the head, and the prayers and work for Orula should be done to open her path. Then the querent's life will improve greatly. In some cases this may indicate a shadow that hangs over the querent from a past life. The work for Orula may remove even this obstacle.

Four/Blank with Five/Blank

This domino is always an indication of severe difficulties in the love life of the female querent. It indicates difficulties with relationships with either sex. The querent who has been extravagant must temper impulses this month, and avoid purchasing anything on impulse.

Four/One

This domino gives a promise of matrimony and economic stability. These changes, or their beginnings, should materialize for the querent before the end of the month. This domino is a good sign of economic prosperity.

This is similar to 3/2, in that it indicates that there is a system and order working in the querent's life. This domino is a good sign for all aspects of the querent's life, as it indicates a steady and continuous influence for good is present throughout the coming month. This is another of the good indications that makes all of the beneficial signs better, and which soften all of the negative signs in a reading. Again, the domino does not speak of health, but it encourages good health in the querent rather than sickness.

Four/Two

Great changes will occur in the querent's life. New things will soon come into every area of life. The querent has thoughts of moving, or of changing jobs. The querent should give an offering of music and food to Chango and Eleggua so that they will help, by allowing the changes in life to be favorable.

The changes that are coming into the life may either be for good or for evil. Offerings are to be given, so that the result of the changes are for the querent's good. Music and dance should be given to Chango, along with 5 red apples, sliced in half and covered with honey. These should be placed as an offering in the querent's house as soon as possible.

Eleggua should receive a candle at the doorway, and if he has not been fed before, he should begin to receive weekly offerings at the doorway for at least three months. In addition, Eleggua should receive 3 shiny pennies at each of the four corners of the city block, or on the corners of the land, that the person lives on. These pennies should be given as an offering to Eshu. The pennies mentioned should be placed every Monday of the month following the reading, even after the nature of the changes in the querent's life have become known. Prayers for the assistance of the Orisha can be made to assist in these changes, making the changes more positive for the person.

Four/Three

This reading is one of blessing and prosperity. It indicates that there will be a victory for the querent, in that he or she will attain desires this month. This domino reveals such positive things as matrimony coming for a single woman, a child coming for the married woman, and marriage for the single man. For the married man there will be the opportunity of a romance with another woman, but this romance will eventually bring great complications into his life.

This domino is an indication of success in all relationships this month, especially those with the love partner. The warning of complications for the married man is one of morality, and for the month in question the complication will probably not surface. If the male querent does get involved with another woman, he should be certain to get a reading every month, to see how his relationship with the woman will progress. It may end in either a divorce or some kind of disaster for him.

It is important for a querent of either sex to realize that choosing the proper mate is more important than simply getting a mate. Many people desire to have a mate without understanding that this is only the first step in forming any true relationship. Counsel the querent to look long and hard before leaping, or the outcome of the leap could be quite negative.

Double Four

This reading indicates that the querent has a number of friends standing by his or her side, friends who will be of assistance. It also indicates that a pleasure trip is coming and the querent will be in the company of friends, and enjoy good times.

■■■

This is a solid indication of material balance and stability in the life of the querent. If it accompanies any other domino that shows change in the life, the amount of change that is ahead is reduced greatly. It also indicates that the person is under the influence of Obatala during the month, and while the influence this month is favorable, the influence should not be exploited. Prayers of thanksgiving should be made by the querent every day this month. No new undertakings should be started this month, unless there are other signs of positive change in the reading. In any case, no major changes should be made—either planned or undertaken.

Five/Blank

Married women should be careful about a man who is coming into their life. This man has evil intentions toward them. This reading also indicates the possibility of public shame, an exposure of their past, and often feelings of disgust. Single women should be very careful in their relations with any married man this month. The querents of either sex must be careful about the possibility of accidents at work. They must use caution in all that they do in the coming month. Querents must make prayers to Obatala, and feed the angel of their head as soon as possible.

This is strong advice to be cautious about situations in the querents' lives. Querents are unable to think with clarity, due to a temporary condition this month. The head must be fed within eight days of the reading. If the querents need a despojo, or if they have not had one for a year or more, they should receive one immediately. This reading is a particularly bad sign for women, as it shows that they are walking on unsafe ground. They are acting through their emotional desires, rather than thinking things out. This domino also amplifies any other warnings directed toward women that may be indicated by the other dominos in the reading. It makes all the other cautions and warnings in this reading that are directed toward women much stronger. All women who receive this domino must be careful of venereal infection and unwanted pregnancy during this month. Men must be very cautious when driving, or when operating any machinery. All querents must be careful to avoid becoming overly tired.

Five/One

This reading shows physical problems with either the stomach or the womb. In some cases, there could be a new addition to the family. There could also be a loss of money, particularly through the temptation to spend more money than the querents have. They should feed Oshun as soon as they can. Querents should not make any holes in the backyard of their home. They should not remove anything that they may find buried in the earth. They must respect Oshun by not eating squash, pumpkin, or other gourd plants. They should wash themselves in a river, or with river water, after feeding the river with honey. This reading is about Oshun.

This reading indicates that there is a problem with Oshun in the querent's home. She is not happy with the querent, but Oshun is not really angry with the querent as yet. At this time she could go either way. Oshun may be said to be indifferent to the querent at the present time. She is withholding her blessing, but she has not displayed her anger. The warnings are present to allow the querent to avoid making Oshun angry. The offering of honey and the bath in the river water are to call the querent to Oshun's attention in a favorable way.

The warnings should be followed for this purpose, as well as following the food taboos mentioned in the reading, for at least the next three months. The reader may wish to discuss certain aspects of Oshun's domain with the querent, to learn how the querent deals with them. This is especially true for the female querent who is not particularly feminine. This may point out any other difficulties to the reader that can be solved through offerings, or even read upon with the coconuts. If the reader cannot arrange for a coconut reading, the querent can obtain a tarot or astrological reading that may provide additional information.

Five/Two

This reading indicates that matrimony, a change of environment, or trips of any kind, are not recommended this month. There are a lot of contraries within the querent's life at this time. An evil spirit is walking with the querent. The querent is not tranquil in his or her heart, and there is a lot of confusion around. The querent should see a medical doctor, and must follow the advice given.

This person must not allow anyone to take charge of his or her life. The querent should listen to the advice given by elders, but must make up his or her own mind, and take responsibility for decisions made. This is not a good month to begin anything new. Maintain usual activities. The querent is instilled with the knowledge of spiritual things. It is time to develop spiritual qualities and receive Aché or spiritual power.

This domino is an indication of problems with the querent's physical health. It is also an indication that the querent may have been "squashed" in life by those who have set themselves over the querent as authorities. This may or may not be the reason for the querent's physical problem. Ogun is within this reading, but he is not speaking. He is only watching the situation. This is not a month for action in any area except the medical, which is required. The querent must have the medical examination completed before receiving any other readings.

Five/Three

This is an excellent reading to get from the dominos. There will be peace and security in the business or at the job this month. Work or position in life will improve this month. A lot of the querent's doubts will be resolved this month.

Notice that this reading does not speak of relationships. While it enhances all other readings about business and economic affairs, it does not deal with the love life at all, so all information in that area must come from other dominos. If there is no other mention made in the reading, it is because that area of life is unimportant this month. This reading is a good indication of favorable stability.

This means the querent should not look for new romance during the month. The querent must be told this, if it is the case. This is the promise of a quiet time, and the symbol is that of a clear spring, flowing gently and softly. There is improvement at the job or relating to working conditions. This reading does not always mean more money, or a better job or position.

Five/Four

This reading promises a marriage that has a lot of love, and a lot of children in it. This month the querent should not invest any money. In general, however, this is a favorable reading for the month.

This reading promises normalcy of the person's desires. The only caution is about loaning or investing money. The querent should refuse to loan any money to any other person. If the querent feels that money should be loaned anyway, the loan must be treated as if it were a gift. It is much better that the querent not part with any money at all. If the querent is married, the marriage will improve this month. If single, the querent may find romance, or may even consider marriage.

■ ■ ■

Double Five

This is an excellent reading for those who desire love. The querent will be triumphant in any new project begun this month. The querent should make an Ebo containing a lot of herbs and leaves for the home.

This is a positive reading and indicates that romance can be expected this month, but the purpose of the Ebo is to bring a lover, so it should be made for that purpose, rather than for any other. If there is a lover or mate in the picture, the querent should make an arrangement of greenery with leaves and herbs for the main room of the home to assist in clearing it of negativity. Ochosi is involved in this reading. So far as other beginnings are concerned, it is a suggestion that success will come from beginning projects. The querent should be asked if any projects are planned. If so, the querent should be encouraged to make a start in whatever it is they have been thinking about.

Six/Blank

This domino indicates that there will be two marriages for the single querent, while for those who are married, there will be a divorce followed by another marriage. The marriage ceremony or the divorce could happen in this month, and it could happen to either the querent, or to one of his or her family members.

∎∎∎

This indicates that there is a marriage in the offing in which the querent will be involved, more than it indicates that the querent will be married during the month. The advice that the marriage is weak applies to one who is married, while the information that the querent will have two marriages applies to the person who is single. This information must be blended with other information from the reading before discussing it in detail with the querent.

For example, the reader might ask, "Have you been married before?" In some cases, more than two marriages are shown, as when the querent has already had two marriages and receives this reading. In this case an additional marriage, or even additional marriages, are in prospect for the querent.

 ## Six/One

There is disappointment, or even disgust, present with members of the immediate family. This includes the parents, sons and daughters, brothers and sisters, or other members of the querent's family. A family member will alienate him- or herself from the querent, or from their family. There may be surprising bad news coming to the querent from afar.

This is a strong warning about the querent's immediate family. The querent should be cautious of them, and be careful of his or her dealings with them. An offering to Yemenja might be required, depending upon the severity of the other dominos in the reading. If there is no other difficulty shown, an offering to Obatala should be made in the form of a glass

∎ ∎ ∎

of water and a white candle, with a prayer on Saturday morning. This should be repeated for eight weeks for the best effect.

Six/Two

If the querent needs surgery, it will be successful. The querent will have success in all undertakings this month. There will be a closer unity in the querent's marriage, along with reconciliation for those who may be separated. There will be good news coming from out of town. There is quiet stability in the querent's life this month.

This reading again has Ogun watching over the person. It is a positive reading and enhances other positive readings that the person receives. This reading may indicate a minor automobile accident in which there are no injuries. It indicates that the result of the accident will be minor or of little consequence. Prayers to Ogun or to Obatala can be made if there are any negative dominos in the reading with this one. The symbol of this domino is that of a man clearing a pathway through a forest or jungle.

Six/Three

This is a particularly good reading for those who are in love. The querent will be victorious in conquering all the obstacles to romance. The querent will have both security and stability in everything planned this month.

This is a very beneficial reading. It moderates all negative readings, and adds greatly to all positive readings.

This is a reading that indicates that the querent will make correct choices this month. It shows that her or his Eleda is strong, and unless it comes with a reading that indicates a feeding of the head, it shows that the head need not be fed this month. If there is a reading that shows that the head must be fed, it means that the feeding will be successful, and that afterward the person will be strong on the chosen path. Following the feeding of the head, this reading will apply. For a man, his plans for the month will be good, and his romantic affairs will go well. For a single woman, it means that she is more likely to be in a favorable position to become attached to the man she is thinking of. For a married woman, there is an indication that the conditions of her marriage will improve.

 ## Six/Four

This reading is a promise of rapid recuperation from evil work that has been done to the querent. (If the querent is sick, or is of a sickly nature, or has been cursed or has had malochia, this is especially applicable.) A marriage ceremony with both money and gifts to the couple is indicated. There are people around who do not wish the querent well, but the querent will triumph. This reading is a strong indication of a positive change in the life.

This reading always promises an unexpected change in the querent's life, especially if it has not been positive to this point. If this domino comes with dominos that indicate offerings must be made, or that work must be done, it means that the condition will be very good after the offerings are made, or after the work is completed. It is a sign of success for the work to be done. The symbol of this domino is the wheel of fortune spinning to a new position in the querent's life. However, this domino is not a guarantee that the positive changes will stay with the querent, unless the person is willing to accept them.

Six/Five

The querent must persist and persevere. It is possible that a radical change will occur, and they may have to begin all over again. Health may be slightly affected, but this condition will not last for long.

This reading is one indicating the work of spiritual forces in the life of the querent. It shows that these forces require that the querent persevere. The querent must keep working toward a goal, regardless of what else is going on. If a change is indicated by the other dominos in the reading, this domino is an indication of a great change. If no change is shown by the other dominos, it means that the time for the change is not yet, but it is coming up fast. This allows the querent to prepare to make this change. In this case, a reading is advised every month until the change physically presents itself, as it may be possible to avert any negative effects of the change, or to improve the conditions of the change, through offerings, charms, or prayers.

Double Six

This is the most important of the domino readings. It says that if the querent picks it twice, he or she must make the saint, or dedicate his or her life to spiritual matters. A person who picks this once must go to see a spiritual teacher (Padrino), and prepare to join a spiritual family. Everything in the future life depends on how the querent respects and cares for the deities who care for the querent. The person will find good health and prosperity once he or she is on the proper path in life. All future life depends on how the querent responds to this reading.

If the person picks this domino twice and does not decide to dedicate him- or herself to spiritual matters, the spiritual life is over, and no more readings may be done for this person. The same is true of the querent who picks it once and refuses to seek a teacher (Padrino). This does not mean that the querent will die; it means that the deities will turn from the querent, and will no longer assist in work, or progress on Earth.

In either case, once any querent states that he or she refuses to follow this reading, the reader can no longer read for the querent any more.

CHAPTER 3

Prayers as Remedies

The following prayers are used as remedies to adverse conditions that are revealed through the reading of the dominos. The reader should have querents copy the appropriate prayers in their own handwriting. Querents should then pray the prayers aloud every day, for at least a month, or as directed by the reading.

There can never be too much praying on this Earth, and we know that sincere prayers are always answered by God, the saints, or the deities to whom they are addressed. The act of praying is in itself sufficient to ward off many negative influences. Praying should be done with great frequency by those who truly wish to spiritualize their lives. Most of the great saints worked hard to turn their lives into a prayer to God; those of us who seek just some of God's blessings should at least pray to our Creator frequently.

Prayer to the Divine Warriors "Los Belli"

Glorious Saint Cosmos and Saint Damian—enforced champions of Jesus Christ—permit me to ask you to adorn me with your profound and divine majesty. I ask that you give to me not only health for my body and spirit, which I desperately require, but that you grant me the glorious terms you have promised after death.

I beg of you, with an eagerness in my soul, that you light in my heart a spark of fire that will burn with the love which the Nazarene possessed within his glorious and precious blood. I ask that you manifest in me a strong and permanent faith, blessed with grace and mercy. I ask for _____ [ask for the blessing desired] _____. This blessing I hope to receive from God. Through my meditations, and my promise to be sincere in gaining the virtues which lead to the devoted spiritual life, I pray that you let this, my blessing, descend upon me.

AMEN

Now, say one "Our Father," one "Hail Mary," and one "Gloria Patri."

■ ■ ■

Other Traditional Christian Prayers

Our Father

Our Father, who art in heaven,
hallowed be Thy Name;
Thy kingdom come,
Thy will be done on earth
        as it is in heaven.
Give us this day our daily bread;
and forgive us our trespasses, as we forgive
those who trespass against us;
and let us not be led into temptation
but deliver us from evil.
For thine is the kingdom, and the power,
and the glory, forever, and ever.

AMEN

■■■

Hail Mary

*Hail Mary, full of grace; the Lord is with thee;
blessed art thou among women, and blessed is the
fruit of thy womb, Jesus. Holy Mary, Mother of
God, pray for us sinners, now and at the hour of
our death.*

AMEN

Gloria Patri

*Glory be to the Father,
and to the Son,
and to the Holy Spirit.
As it was in the beginning,
is now, and ever shall be,
world without end.*

AMEN

Prayer for Peace
(of Saint Francis of Assisi)

This is the Prayer of St. Francis of Assisi; it may be made to him on a daily basis for three months to remedy any of the things that work against you, or as directed in the readings.

Lord, make me an instrument of your peace;
Where there is hatred, let me sow love;
Where there is injury, pardon;
Where there is discord, union;
Where there is doubt, faith;
Where there is despair, hope;
Where there is darkness, light;
And where there is sadness, joy.
O divine master, grant that I may not
*   so much seek to be consoled, as to console;*
To be understood as to understand;
To be loved, as to love;
For it is in giving that we receive.
It is in pardoning that we are pardoned,
And it is in dying that we are born
*   to eternal life.*

AMEN

■■■

Prayer to the Sacred Heart of Jesus

This prayer may be used when prayers to Obatala are asked for in the readings. It must be prayed every day for at least eight days.

O Sacred Heart of Jesus, filled with infinite love, broken by my ingratitude, pierced by my sins, yet loving me still: accept the consecration that I make to you of all that I am and all that I have. Take every faculty of my soul and body. Draw me, day by day, nearer to your Sacred Heart, and there, as I can bear the lesson, teach me your blessed ways.

AMEN

■ ■ ■

Prayer to Saint Michael, the Archangel

This prayer can be used by Christians instead of the prayers to Eleggua when prayers to him are called for in the readings. Prayers should be made every Monday morning for at least a month, but it is always better if they are made for three months.

St. Michael, the Archangel, defend us in the day of battle; be our safeguard against the evil and snares of the devil. May God rebuke the devil, we humbly pray, and do you, O prince of the heavenly host, by the power of God, cast Satan into Hell, and equally banish all of the other evil spirits who prowl through the world, seeking the ruin of souls.

AMEN

∎∎∎

The Anima Christi of Saint Ignatius Loyola

This is one of the many prayers that may be said on a daily basis as prayers to God.

Soul of Christ, sanctify me.
Body of Christ, save me.
Blood of Christ, inebriate me.
Water from the side of Christ, Wash me.
Passion of Christ, Strengthen me.
O good Jesus, hear me.
Within your wounds hide me.
Permit me not to be separated from you.
From the malignant enemy, defend me.
In the hour of my death, call me,
And bid me come to you.
That, with your saints, I may praise you.
Forever and ever.

AMEN

■ ■ ■

An Offering of the Self
(Saint Ignatius Loyola)

This prayer should be prayed by the person who receives the Double Six domino to resign themselves to following the spiritual path, to which they have been called by the reading.

Take, O Lord, into your hands my entire liberty, my memory, my understanding, and my will. All that I am and have, you have given me, and I surrender them to you, to be so disposed in accordance with your holy will.

Give me your love and your grace; with these I am rich enough and desire nothing more.

AMEN

Prayer to Saint Alejo

This prayer may be used whenever the person feels a dark shadow around, or whenever negativity or evil is directed at the person according to the reading. This prayer should be written out by the person and prayed whenever it is needed, in addition to praying it every morning and every evening. Ideally, this prayer should be prayed at sunrise and sunset every day of the month that is covered by any reading indicating darkness or warning against darkness in the life of the person.

Glorious Saint Alejo, you who have received the power to take away all evil that may surround the Lord, I ask you to take my enemies far away from me.

Take me away from Devils,

Take me away from Liars,

Take me away from Sinners,

and finally, I pray that you take those who would harm me away from me.

Place me so far from those evil ones that they will never see me.

Take away from me all those who have evil thoughts and wish to harm me.

Bring me closer to the Lord so that with His Divine Grace, I will be covered with goodness.

AMEN

Prayer to Saint Anthony of Padua at His Festival

This prayer can be used on the Festival Day of St. Anthony (June 13th) in addition to any other prayers that are prescribed by the reading for any person who is in need of justice. It should also be prayed on that date by any single man looking for a mate, by any person who has been accused of a crime, and by anyone who feels that others are working against him or her. Note that this prayer may only be used on the saint's festival date, June 13th.

O, sweetest Saint Anthony, my Guide and Protector. What a good time this is to receive your mercy and forgiveness, now that the Church is celebrating the sacred name of Saint Anthony, and being in his arms and finding them filled with love, what could you deny us, your humble servants, you who are our intermediary?

Let the Holy Fountain of your mercies be shed upon us all.

Let the doors of Heaven be open by means of the Great Saint Anthony, so that we may receive the grace of our savior on this day.

Turn your glorious face to us, Dear Lord, who are devotees of Saint Anthony, and who, trusting in his help, promise to reform our lives, through the confession of our sins, our obedience to sacred laws, and by our showing infinite love to the Blessed Mary. Let us be filled with hope and love which will give us the strength of heart to defeat the spirit of darkness. So Divine Father, as we hear the melodies that the Church intones today in honor of Saint Anthony, raise your almighty hand and forgive us, and bless us in our needs.

AMEN

■ ■ ■

Prayer to Saint Barbara Against Temptation

St. Barbara is viewed, in the Yoruba African pantheon, as the feminine side of Chango. This prayer should be used by women who are single, and who are indicated by the reading to be in a negative relationship, or in temptation of entering into one. These women should pray this prayer at least five times during the month of the reading, but they should also pray the prayer whenever they feel sexual temptation within themselves. The prayer may also be used by men to avoid temptation, especially temptation from immoral women. They should pray it every day, especially when the reading indicates that they are likely to be entering into a negative relationship during that month.

Magnificent and eternal God, we admire your saints, especially the glorious Virgin and Martyr, Saint Barbara. We give thanks for those who were worthy of your intercession and were freed from all evil, helping them in their hour of need, not permitting them to die without receiving the Holy Sacraments and granting and assuring them that their petitions had been heard. I beg everything by the merits of the dear Saint Barbara. Give me strength to resist temptations and to know my own faults. And so to be worthy of that sacred and Holy Virgin, especially in my hour of death, fortified with the Holy Sacraments and by them, and with the intercession of Saint Barbara, happy in your company with you and with your glory, where you live and reign in Heaven.

AMEN

Say one "Our Father" and one "Hail Mary."

■ ■ ■

Prayer of the Door

This prayer is to be made when leaving the house every day. To that extent it is to Eleggua, as both the door and the door-keeper of the Yoruba pantheon. It is also a prayer to the person's own guardian angel, as is shown in the body of the prayer itself. This prayer can be made every day to strengthen the connection between the person and his or her guardian angel.

Divine Providence, you who were the author of all that I believe, without whose will nothing is moved. I think of you in my moments of uncertainty, so that you will guide me and protect me from evil and envious spirits. Guide me, and guide my spirit. If any of my enemies, because of envy, raises their hands to hurt me, or says anything to harm me, turn aside their hands and their evil thoughts and have them repent of their errors against me and have them ask my pardon. And I will forgive them and beg God for their salvation.

Guardian Angel, do not let me, because I am innocent, become a victim or be blamed for sins I have not committed for the satisfaction of my enemies. In the name of The All Powerful God, I beg my Guardian Angel and the spirits that protect me, that I be freed from all bad influences and temptations, and that the spirits of light will save me forever.

Great Power, may this prayer protect me from my material and spiritual enemies, and I pray that your Divine Grace shield me with your hand.

AMEN

Prayer to Saint Expeditus

St. Expeditus is prayed to to bring those things that are required in a hurry. In the Yoruba pantheon, he is represented by the humble but active aspect of Eleggua or Eshu, who is the messenger of the Orisha. Prayers to him to assist in the fulfillment of other prayers are always valuable, and when this is desired, the prayer to St. Expeditus should be made.

Oh glorious Martyr and protector, Saint Expeditus, having faith in your great merits and above all in the precious blood of Jesus Christ. We humbly beg of you that you reach out to us and send us from God the virtues necessary to make us good and pious. Studying and practicing your virtues we can exercise them and follow your example here in life so that we can deserve the merits of glory hereafter.

AMEN

Prayer for Peace in the Home

Prayers of this kind, and prayers to either St. Agnus or St. Martha, may be made whenever a forecast of dissension in the home is found in the reading. The person who receives the warning reading should make the prayer every day for at least nine days. A novena to St. Martha or to St. Agnes can also be made, using a seven-day-candle lit specifically for her.

Lord, I am one of the mortals who sometimes walks blindly down my road, by succeeding, I will be able to lead and not follow. But all is hopeful because of your greatness. I want peace as much as I want bread in my home, as the peace of the poor. I pray for peace of the tyrants and for my enemies. I pray for peace that shines in our minds and groups us together. As we all come from the same fountain, let us have peace so that with our spirits resolved in peace, we can be transported to the world of the beautiful.

Oh sacred peace that flies from our hearts as the dollar flies from our pockets, do not abandon us; we know that the spirit of God is the spirit of peace.

Cover us with the veil of your grace and your own magnificence. Glory to God in the highest and peace among men of good will.

AMEN

■ ■ ■

Prayer to Saint Jude Tadeo

St. Jude Tadeo, also known as St. Jude Thadaeus, is the patron saint of those in desperate straits, those who believe they have no hope pray to him for relief from their problems. This prayer should be used by people who have a negative reading, particularly those who receive the Blank/Blank domino in a reading.

The prayer is said, along with the additional prayers as they are listed near the end. Then the specific request to St. Jude is prayerfully made. When the prayer is answered, it is often appropriate to post in a newspaper a notice of thanks to St. Jude for any favors received.

I believe, oh glorious apostle Saint Jude, that you are in Heaven in the favor of Jesus Christ, contemplating divine peace, possessing God, being absorbed in a thousand delights that constitute your eternal happiness.

You returned the graces of Jesus with constant loyalty and you loved Him with all your heart.

Your devotion made you fly to instill in the heart of the multitudes, the productive seed of truth of the Protector of the despaired.

In payment for so much courage and for your most worthy works, sinners spilled your blood with insane cruelty.

Give me the grace to repent for my sins, to live with His friendship, to imitate your example, and to die fulfilling my duties as a Christian.

[Say three "Our Fathers," three "Hail Marys,"
and one "Glory to the Father"]

Grant it to me. If what I ask from God does not oppose my eternal salvation, give it to me, as I entreat you with veneration and faith.

AMEN

■ ■ ■

Prayer to Saint Lazarus

St. Lazarus is viewed by the Yoruba as the Spirit of the Earth. His Yoruba name means "Lord of the Earth." In some cases he is seen as the spirit of illness, poverty, and want. Those who have physical problems should pray to him, and ask him to relieve their difficulty. As he is a very powerful deity he is difficult to appease, but it may be done through sincere prayer. The prayer below should be repeated three times each day for seventeen consecutive days. At the end of that time a candle should be lit to St. Lazarus, and the written prayer placed underneath the candleholder.

Oh Holy and Glorious Saint Lazarus, sustained by Saint Martha and Saint Mary; I call on you, oh loving and forever living spirit of grace, with the same faith and love that Jesus called at the door of His tomb from where He left alive in three glorious days after He was buried without showing any sign of impurity or imperfection.

Therefore, I as a believer also call upon you at the door of your holy spirit so that with the same faith that God instilled in you, grant me what I ask for in this prayer . . .

Invoking for him the incomparable love with which God asked from you with your holy brothers and the great humility and resignation with which you knew how to suffer the pains and miseries which you suffered during all your life on Earth, I ask in the name of God the Father, God the Son, and God the Holy Ghost.

AMEN

Say one "Our Father," one prayer to St. Martha, and two "Hail Marys." Repeat this three times, meaning, do the prayer for St. Lazarus, one "Our Father," (p. 55) one prayer to St. Martha (p. 70), and two "Hail Marys" (p. 56), and then do it all again, and again.

■ ■ ■

Prayer to Saint Martha

Glorious and Blessed St. Martha, guardian of the home, bless my home that it be a refuge from the cares of the world for my family and myself. Aid my home in becoming one that is full of peace and love. I pray that the real presence of Christ be installed here, and that there be no dissension nor deceit between the members of our family.

AMEN

■ ■ ■

Prayer to Saint Martin

This prayer should be used when the reading indicates the querent will have a threat regarding chastity in the coming month. The person who receives the reading should pray it every day.

By the sign of the Holy Cross, free us from our enemies in the name of the Father, the Son, and the Holy Ghost. Amen.

Oh, merciful God, who gave us Saint Martin as a perfect model of humility and charity, who, without looking at his own condition, faithfully served until gloried in God's kingdom with the angels.

It was you, Saint Martin, who lived only for God, and for good works. It was you, who were so understanding to all unfortunate and poor people. It was you who so piously attended those who admired virtue and who recognized divine power. They praised you to God.

Make us feel the effects of your great charity; bring us closer to God, who faithfully rewarded your merits with eternal glory.

AMEN

Prayer to Saint Michael
The Archangel Against Enemies

This prayer is used whenever there is an indication in the reading that the person has enemies. The person should immediately make this prayer after lighting a candle to St. Michael, the Archangel, the Yoruba Eshu. This prayer can be said whenever the querent feels the force of the enemy around. It will give strong protection against any enemy.

Saint Michael Archangel, as you are the person in charge of all of the works in the world, I implore you at this solemn hour and day to seize this time so that you will see the light, candle, and work. Sorcery and corruption remove yourselves from my body. The flesh and blood of my enemy should treat me well.

Let my enemies suffer as Jesus suffered on the tree of the cross—bitterness, torment, kicks, and slaps—like those he suffered.

Let them go into a desolate world.

Let them take the three falls that Jesus took until my enemy comes to my home asking pardon for his sins. The stars in heaven bear witness to my pleas.

AMEN

Say three "Apostles' Creed."

■■■

Prayer to Our Lady of Perpetual Help

This general prayer to the Blessed Mother for assistance may be made at any time. In the Yoruba pantheon, this would be considered a prayer to the aspect of the Mother Orisha, Yemenja, who lives in the forest with the Orisha Ogun, working alongside him.

Oh, most Holy Virgin Mary, by means of inspiring our entire confidence, you wanted to take the sweet name of Our Lady of Perpetual Help. I implore you that you help and protect me everywhere at all times, in my temptations, after my falls, in my difficulties, in all miseries of life, and especially at the hour of my death. Give me, oh merciful Mother, the thought and habit of coming to you at all times. For I am sure that if I implore you with sincerity, you won't forget to help me. Please reach for me this grace of graces, the faith of asking you always with the faith of a child, so with the virtue of this faithful prayer.

"I can obtain your perpetual help and final perseverance."

Bless me, oh, Sweet Savior and Benevolent Mother, and pray for me. Oh Mother of Perpetual Help, favor me with your mighty help which I ask for without ceasing.

AMEN

■■■

The Prayer to the Worker

This prayer may be used by anyone who has difficulty at work. It is especially useful for the person who works irregularly at whatever comes to hand. It should be prayed daily when the reading indicates that there are difficulties with the work situation.

Jesus, Mary, and Joseph, when I get up I ask for work, health, and progress. Joseph, the working man, come with me when I go to obtain my bread with the sweat of my brow; the three Angels of Jesus, come with me, and talk for me when I go to solicit work. Saint Joaquin, Saint Peter, Saint Michael, I also ask. I ask the Seven Powers that I pray to to help me through Jesus, Mary, and Joseph. Oh, my God, give me bread if you think I am deserving; if not, it will be your will that decides my luck. I have refused my own brother bread when I had the opportunity to help him, be it through work or through charity, pardon me for my faults and ignorances in having failed your law.

AMEN

Say three "Our Fathers" and three "Hail Marys."

■ ■ ■

Prayer to the Seven African Powers

The Seven African Powers are the seven principal deities of the Yoruba Orisha pantheon. They are usually related directly to seven saints in the Roman Catholic Calendar of Saints. The prayer to the Seven African Powers may be used whenever prayers to the Orisha, or the feeding of elekes, is indicated in a reading.

Oh, Seven Powers of Africa, you who are the divinities among the divinities, who work at the behest of the living God, the Creator of the universe, I humbly kneel before your blessed picture to pray for your help and intercession in my life. I ask that God, my loving Father who made and protects all creation, living and dead, and that you, the Seven Powers of Africa and the world, accede to my prayer and give me the spiritual peace and progress I seek.

God, you who are my supply and protection, through the action of your will and the Seven Powers, give me material success and cleanse from my house and my path the dangers and evils which torment me. Let them be gone from me that they never torment me again.

My heart tells me that my prayer is just, and that my path is open to the benefits and blessings I seek. I ask that God grant my prayer for the intercession of the Seven Powers, and for their help and guidance to me in my daily life.

Listen to me, Chango . . . Aid me, Yemanja . . . Do not forsake me, Ogun . . . Intercede for me, Eleggua . . . Hear me, Oshun . . . Look at me with favor, Obatala . . . Act with favor to me, Orula.

Grant what I ask that it be manifested in my life, through the meditation of the Seven African Powers. Olofi, bless me that I may forever be blessed.

AMEN

∎∎∎

CHAPTER 4

Making a Novena

A novena is a series of nine prayers made for a specific intention. As usually practiced today, nine candles are burned, one at a time, on nine different days or nights. As each candle is lit, the prayer request is made, earnestly, sincerely, and with fervor and piety.

The prayer request should be hand-written and placed under the candle before it is lighted. Many people who make a novena copy their request on a piece of paper, which they place under the candle. The prayer is then prayed from the original paper, placed before the candle.

Any request that a person desires may be made in this way. And the novena may be made on nine consecutive days, nine of the same days of the week (as on nine Thursdays), or on nine of the same days of the month, depending on desire of the petitioner.

Any of the prayers presented in the previous chapter may be used in a novena, especially if the reading indicates that difficulties lie ahead. Many who have used the novena in prayer feel it is the best way to obtain answers to their prayers.

An example of the need for a novena, let us suppose that a man receives a reading that indicates troubles ahead for him on on the job, or the possibility of an accident. He might wish to avoid these difficulties, realizing that he needs the job to keep bread on the table and a home for his family. The suggestions of remediations and offerings to the Orisha made in the reading may not seem to be enough to quiet his mind so he decides to make a novena, to further quiet fears and to ensure that the difficulties promised by the reading do not come to pass.

Now let us suppose that this person is an ordinary worker and that he has no skill except for the work of his hands to produce income for the family. In this case, he might wish to make a Novena of the Prayer to the Worker (page 74). He would purchase nine candles, and pray the Prayer to the Worker after lighting the candle. He would do this every morning for nine days, allowing the candle to burn out.

In the case of someone faced with a difficult situation—one that seems to be impossible to correct—a novena made to St. Jude would be effective. In this case the person would light the candle to St. Jude on nine consecutive days, and make the prayer before it, allowing the candle to burn out.

A novena is an especially strong appeal to the Orisha, saints, or forces of the universe. It almost never is allowed to go unheard or unfulfilled.

■ ■ ■

Ebos: Spells and Remedies
(For Requests to, and the Propitiation of, the Orishas)

The African Yoruba tradition has any number of spells and offerings that may be given to the many Orisha or deities of the tradition to ward off negative conditions of various kinds. In addition, there are also offerings to encourage positive conditions to come into the life. The general term for these offerings are Ebo's, although they are also known by several other names, such as *despatchos*.

The actual practice of the Yoruba African tradition is highly individualized. Thus each Pi de Santo may see things a bit differently than his neighbor Pi de Santo. Unlike the Roman Catholic religion, which has given a great deal to the Yoruba African practices in the Western Hemisphere, there is no central authority for the religion. In this way, each family is more or less on their own in the way they practice the religion, under the direction of the Pi de Santo. Although there are great similarities between the various groups, there are also differences between them. Ever since the introduction of Islam to the Yoruba, about 900 C.E., and the later introduction of Christianity, about 1390, the religion has absorbed whatever it could use from any source available to it. The result is one of the most rapidly growing, and fertile religious and magical practices known today.

Thus these Ebos, or offerings to the deities, are all well tested and frequently used in the Yoruba practice. The list below is far from complete; there are thousands more available to the initiate or worshiper of a family in the practice. However, the following list is complete enough so that any-

■■■

one using this book will have a wide selection of basic spells and remedies from which to choose.

Special care has been taken to indicate just how these Ebos should be prepared, and what is to be done with anything remaining from them.

A Bath for Purification from
Negative Influences: To Obatala

Mix together the whites of 8 eggs and some shavings from a bar of coconut oil soap. Add 1 teaspoon coconut oil and 1/2 cup water. Shake this mixture in a jar until it is well mixed. Now add this mixture to a tub of cool or warm (but never hot) water. Enter the tub and immerse yourself 8 times while praying to Obatala to remove all negative influences from your life. Remain in the tub 8 minutes. When you leave the tub, allow yourself to dry in the air, so that there will be some of the solution remaining on your body until the next time you bathe.

A Bath for Greater Energy for Your Work: Oshumerae

Make the same recipe as you use for the Purification bath. After shaking the mixture in a bottle, add 1 tablespoon corn starch and shake it again to mix it thoroughly. Now add this mixture to a tub of cool or warm water (but never hot water). Enter the tub and immerse yourself 7 times while praying to Oshumerae to give you the energy that you need to do your work on Earth. You may mention a specific project if you wish. Immerse yourself in the water 9 times, and stay in the tub at least 9 minutes. When you leave the tub allow yourself to air dry, as mentioned earlier. You should sleep with this bath on your skin for the best results.

A Bath to Clean Yourself from Being Fouled by Anyone or Anything: To Obatala

Take 8 white eggshells, with the membrane inside them removed. Let them dry and grind them into a fine white powder. Add a small pinch of salt, and 1 teaspoon coconut oil. Place this mixture in a cool bath, and wash your entire body in the bath with a bar of pure Castile soap. While you are washing yourself, pray to Obatala to remove all negativity in your life, and keep all negative influences away from you. Scrub your body thoroughly in the tub. When you leave the tub, thank Obatala for cleansing you. Then you may dry yourself and go about your business.

An Offering for Eleggua

Mix together about 1 cup yellow cornmeal, 3 tablespoons honey, and enough water to make a stiff paste. Form this mixture into three approximately equal sized balls. Place the balls and 6 pennies into a small paper bag. Wipe the bag containing these ingredients all over your nude body. Once you have dressed, place the bag at a crossroads; then pray at the same crossroads that Eleggua look on you with favor, assisting you in making progress on your path in life.

An Offering for Chango:
To Open Opportunities for Yourself

Take 6 bottles of beer to a place where there are several large rocks or boulders. Open each of the bottles of beer, and pour

■ ■ ■

about a third of the beer from each bottle onto the rocks. Set the bottles with the remaining beer upright near the rocks. Now pray to Chango to open up opportunities for you. You may state just what kind of opportunities you want, if you wish to do so. As an example, you may ask for opportunities for a good job, or for a good relationship. When you have finished your prayer, walk away and put the entire episode out of your mind.

An Offering for Chango:
For a Woman to Find a Lover

If the dominos say that a lover may present himself for you in the coming month, the following Ebo will encourage this to happen.

Obtain 5 red candles and 1 ripe red apple. Get a tape of dance music that you like. Now place the 5 candles on a dresser and cut the apple into quarters. Cover the apple quarters with honey. Disrobe and put on the dance music. Now light the 5 red candles and dance as the music plays and pray as you dance that Shango send you a man to become your lover.

• • •

There are a number of other techniques for spiritual cleansing in *Spiritual Cleansing* by Draja Mickaharic This book is also published by Samuel Weiser. Other techniques and Ebos will be given as needed, by your Pi de Santo. If you have no Pi de Santo, you should read *Spiritual Cleansing* before beginning to read for others.

Glossary of Unfamiliar Words

Asavache: A charm made by a priest that is given to a person for a specific purpose. It often breaks, or is lost, when its purpose is completed. These asavache charms are usually inexpensive, costing up to $25.00, but rarely more.

St. Barbara: St. Barbara is taken as the Christian representation of Chango. She is viewed as less macho, as Chango is supposed to be the ideal male, and so he is very macho indeed. Her symbols of the Tower and Lightning are understood by the Yoruba as symbols of Chango's rulership. Prayers are made to St. Barbara in place of prayers to Chango by those who feel more at home with the more feminine nature of St. Barbara than the rough masculine concept of divine justice that Chango represents.

Caracoles: The name of the system of reading cowry shells that is part of the corpus of Ifa, the African geomantic oracle.

These shells may only be read by an initiated priest of the Yoruba religion. There are various levels of readings that may be obtained by the querent, as there are various levels of readers. The senior level of reader in the both Yorubaland and the Americas is the Babalawo, known as the Father of the Oracle.

Chango: The Yoruba deity of divine justice, known as the owner of fire; he was a worldly king, as well as a great magician. Chango is viewed as the thunderstorm, and the lightning that comes with it. Those who are killed when struck by lightning are said to be sacred to him. Chango has some correspondence with the planetary spirit of Jupiter. His priests are expected to have sex with almost all the women who come to them for consultation. This sexual surrender is viewed by both the priest and the woman as giving themselves to the deity Chango, and is not ever considered to be an immoral action.

Coconut Reading: The reading of the coconut, given by one who is either a priest in one of the practices of the Yoruba pantheon, or is studying the religion and is on the way to becoming a priest. The reading is quite complex and can be amazingly accurate. It is accomplished with five pieces of coconut.

Despojo: A spiritual cleansing, often given to a querent by the reader, or in the case of a more complex and advanced cleansing, by a Pi de Santo, who is always a priest. The better, and more complex, spiritual cleansings require that

■■■

the person being cleaned provide at least some of the materials used in the cleansing. Many of the simple spiritual cleansings are simply done by the person who needs it. In this case, the reader or the priest will instruct the person about what he or she is to do. Prepared baths can be used for regular spiritual cleansing by most people. The extent of the despojo, or spiritual cleansing, that is required is usually given in the reading.

Divination: Any one of the many means of "learning the will of the divine" through following the rules of a particular system of divination. Astrology, numerology, and tarot reading, are some of the better known systems of divination in the West. For the most part, European systems of divination are used only to read or predict the immediate future; while almost all African, and many Eastern, systems of divination are used to both read the future and control or improve both the present and the immediate future. Some systems of divination are initiatory, in that the reader must be an initiate, or even a priest, of a particular magical or religious practice to be able use the system of divination.

Ebo: An offering, spell, or other action done to obtain a particular effect. Frequently it is done in the name of a deity. It may be something that is done along with prayers to an Orisha or deity to obtain a particular effect in the life of a person. It may also be an arrangement of herbs gathered or prepared by a priest (ideally a priest of Osainyin) that are used for various reasons, such as to heal a physical condition, to protect from evil influences, or for some other reason. In some

∎∎∎

cases, the herbs are gathered and made into an Ebo to place in the house of a person to honor a particular Orisha, or a deity who is important to the person at that time. There are a number of Ebos that may be used in conjunction with domino readings given earlier in this book.

Eleggua—Eshu: The Yoruba equivalent of Mercury, the messenger god who must be propitiated to carry the message accurately. The ruler of the crossroads, he is represented by the hinges on the door of the house. He is the divine troublemaker, much as is Loki in the Norse pantheon, but no one can do without Eleggua, as he rules the principle of motion. Eleggua is given proprietary offerings of sweets, which he likes very much indeed. His day is Monday, his number is 6, and his colors are red and black. Readers often counsel their querents to avoid wearing red and black together, as this is said to attract Eleggua in an unfavorable way.

Elekes or **Elekas:** The necklaces of beads that are a part of the process of initiation, protection, and spiritual growth in the Yoruba religion. They are given to people for various things, such as protection, balance, and so forth. They must be given by a priest to the person receiving them. Once given, they must be respected by the person wearing them. Usually there are specific rules for their care that are given by the priest to the person receiving them. These same appealing necklaces are also the indication of one who is a priest in the Yoruba religious practices. However, the necklaces given to the student or querent are not at all the same as the ones given to the priest at his initiation.

■ ■ ■

Feeding the Head: This is done to strengthen a person's mind and to clear or improve their thinking. This is a ritual that is usually done by a priest. It may be done by the person themselves, or the reader may do it for the querent in some circumstances. The more urgently the reading seems to require this work, the more likely it is that it should be done by a priest.

Geomancy: Any one of a number of divination systems based on making marks on the earth—interpreting the results of casting shells, stones, arrows, and other similar practices. Most of the African geomantic divination systems, such as Ifa, are ultimately derived from the Arabic practice of "Ramal," which is divination from the casting of sand.

Ibeji: The divine twins are said to be equivalent to the astrological sign Gemini, or of the stars Castor and Pollox, or to the twins Sts. Cosmos and Damian. The Ibeji are the Yoruba equivalent of these famous twins of antiquity.

Jimaguas: The deity of merchants and traders, a person of business. In the Yoruba pantheon she is not a very important deity. Trade in Yorubaland, as with the Europeans of the Middle Ages, is considered not a suitable occupation for men of worth. The marketplace is owned by Eleggua, but the business transactions themselves are carried on by Jimaguas. In some cases Jimaguas is viewed by the Yoruba as a middle-aged market woman who shrewdly counts out her profits at the end of the day.

■ ■

Los Belli—the Warriors: A group of deities or Orisha in the Yoruba religion who act to protect those who are placed under their care. These are usually Ochosi (St. Sebastian), Chango (St. Barbara), Ogun (St. John, the Baptist), and Eleggua (St. Michael, the Archangel). The divine twins are the Christian equivalent of this group, as they were warriors who were executed by the pagan Romans when it was discovered that they were Christians.

Malochia: The Evil Eye, which afflicts people with pains and brings errors into their life. It is given to people by those who are envious or jealous of them. Malochia is the most common, and most frequent, spiritually derived physical complaint. It has been shown that the evil eye is a real energy that proceeds from the eyes of the sender, who is only rarely conscious of his or her evil act. Malochia is the cause of much pain and suffering in the world.

Oba: One of the three wives of Shango, she is a modest woman whose hair always covers her ears. She is not as sexual as the other wives of Shango. She is often prayed to and asked to tame the passion of wives with roving eyes.

Obatola or **Obatala:** The principal deity of the Yoruba pantheon on Earth, he is also known as the God of Gods, or the Lord of the White Cloth. Obatala rules purity and spiritual growth. His numbers are 8 and 16 and his color is white. He is said to be the equivalent of Christ, and the chief of the Yoruba pantheon of Orisha.

■■■

Ochosie: The Yoruba hunting deity. He lives in the woods and hunts game. He is appealed to for success in hunting, as well as for finding a lover.

Ogun: The Yoruba deity of war, he is very much like Mars. He rules surgeons and craftsmen as well as all who use knives, metal workers, and mechanics of every kind. Ogun is a warrior and a hunter who prefers to live apart from civilization. His metal is iron, his number 7, and his colors are brown and black.

Olofi: The supreme God in the Yoruba pantheon, the same as God the Father Almighty in Christianity. The Yoruba view him as having given over the day-to-day rulership of Earth to the lesser deities (the Orisha) that he had created for this purpose, as his administrators on Earth.

Orisha: The Yoruba word for "Gods," it is best translated into English as "deity." These are forces of the universe that were created by God to be in charge of certain of the affairs of Earth, and of many of the affairs of human beings. Each of the Orisha, or Orisa, have their own realm of power and action. They are all very powerful and have great abilities in their own sphere.

Orula: The owner of the Oracle of Ifa, the principal oracle of the Yoruba peoples. Orula is the deity of divination. All divination, of every kind, is said to come from his hand. His colors are yellow and green alternating, his numbers are 8 and 16.

■ ■ ■

Osainyin: The Yoruba deity of herbs, he is said to be a powerful magician whose priests gather herbs and make charms from them called Ebos. He is the herbal healer of the Yoruba pantheon, and so rules medicine. Because of his closeness to nature, he is said to be similar to St. Francis Assisi. His symbol is the rooster, which sits on top of his greatest protective charm, the Cup of Osainyin.

Oshumerae: The rainbow deity, she is the symbol of the universal life force that permeates all of the creation, keeping it alive. She is symbolized by the rainbow boa constrictor, who renews her life by shedding her skin.

Oshun: The Yoruba equivalent of Venus, she is the goddess of fresh water and rules the fish in streams, rivers, and lakes. Oshun is one of the three wives of Chango, and is concerned with all affairs of the heart. She likes honey, which must be tasted before it is offered to her. Yellow is her color, 5 is her number. She is said to be the owner of gold, which she likes very much. She also is said to rule copper, fine cooking, perfume, and beautiful clothing.

Oya: One of the three wives of Chango, she is also known as a magician. She is seen by the Yoruba as a powerful and strong willed, but very sensual, woman. There is no true European deity correspondence to her, although she is slightly similar to Athena. Her number is said to be 9 and her colors black and white. No candles are ever lighted in her honor, as she is said to use them against the people who light them for her. She is said to live in the wind that comes before the thunderstorm. She is symbolized by the iron fence that is around the cemetery.

Pi de Santo: The Father of the Saint—the person who is the head of the "Family" of initiate priests and priestesses of a group that practices the Yoruba religion, in one of the many forms in which it is practiced in the Americas. The Pi de Santo becomes the spiritual father of those whom he initiates, or who join his religious family. Also known in some areas as the Padrino, the terms are actually interchangeable.

St. Barbara, *see* **Barbara**.

Shango—Chango: The principle of divine justice, he is seen as a rough warrior king who maintains justice in his kingdom with an iron hand. Having three wives, and many frequent casual sexual affairs, he is the macho male personified. St. Barbara is his feminine aspect. His colors are red and white, his number is 5. His favorite offering is stewed okra, and red apples quartered with honey poured over them. Red candles are burned as offerings to him.

Yemenja: The Yoruba equivalent of the Virgin Mary, she is the Mother Goddess of the Yoruba. She is said to own the ocean, with all of its treasure. Thus she rules salt water. Her colors are all of the shades of the ocean, from sea green to dark blue. Her number is 7. Her rulership of the Moon has been given her by the South American practices of the Yoruba religion. Yemenja rules childbirth, the parenting of the mother, and mothers to be.

■ ■ ■

Index

Index

■ ■ ■

■ ■ ■

■ ■ ■

About the Author

Carlos G. y Poenna was born in Cuba and came to the United States following the Castro Revolution. He has been involved with the practice of Santeria since he was young, and was initiated into Santeria in 1965. A graduate in education of the University of Havana, Cuba, y Poenna presently teaches science and chemistry at the secondary school level in Miami. He is an active member of a large Santeria family there. This is his first book.